Mother as Conjunction

Some names and identifying details in these essays have been changed to protect the privacy of individuals.

Mother as Conjunction

For permissions and information on ordering books, contact operations@smallharborpublishing.com.

Cover art: Leslie F. Miller, "She's Funny Looking"
Cover design: Brianna Protesto
Interior design: Claire Eder
Publisher: Allison Blevins
Executive Editor: Kristiane Weeks-Rogers
Managing Editor: Bianca Dagostino

MOTHER AS CONJUNCTION
ERIN MURPHY
ISBN 978-1-957248-62-2
Harbor Editions,
an imprint of Small Harbor Publishing
Special thanks to: The Wild & Precious Life Series and Kristin Vandeventer

Mother as Conjunction

Lyric Essays

Erin Murphy

Harbor Editions
Small Harbor Publishing

Contents

Mother as Conjunction

Re-entry

On the first hit by the first batter in the first inning of our first game since the start of the pandemic, a ball soars over the outfield wall and into the face of a boy beside us. One minute we're sipping beer in minor league seats—the next, we hear a woman scream.

***

When astronauts return to earth, gravity grabs them like a mugger, dragging their bodies through a furnace pounded by sledgehammers. Then the parachute opens and rocks them gently like a swing.

***

When I was in fifth grade, a man eager to date our mother invited her, my four year old brother, and me on his business trip to L.A. He took us to a taping of my favorite show, *The Dating Game*, in which a bachelorette quizzes eligible men hidden from her view. We sat on the top row of bleacher seats against a brick wall. On the first question of the first round, my brother leaned back against the wall, which turned out to be a flimsy trompe l'oeil curtain. He fell twenty feet, landing face first on a concrete floor.

***

A soft landing for astronauts isn't soft at all. It's more like a head-on collision with a Mack truck. They brace for it by jamming their tongues behind their teeth. And then: *Bam.*

***

Blood spread under my brother's motionless body. My mother tried to jump after him. Other audience members held her back.

***

Back on earth after space travel, everything is heavy: your watch, your own hands. What's yours is no longer yours.

***

Next week my husband and I will return to campus after teaching online for eighteen months. We'll lecture in masks, reading our students' expressions through their eyes. Maybe we've grown too fond of orbiting our old lives.

***

The night my brother fell, I sat alone in the ER waiting room not knowing if he was alive or dead. Sometime past midnight, the businessman brought me vending-machine Doritos. He seemed irritated.

***

After the ball hits the boy, he looks stunned, probably in shock. His cheek turns a deep maroon, like Bordelaise sauce seeping through cheesecloth. *Possible fracture, concussion,* says the EMT. He asks the boy's age. *Eight,* the mother says, and then: *I mean nine—today's his birthday. It's his birthday,* she repeats, as if this should shield him.

***

Somewhere in a Hollywood warehouse there's an unedited recording of a young woman in yellow bell-bottoms asking a prospective mate if he's a morning person or night owl. Before the man can answer, before the neon-blur ambulance ride, before the ICU and MRI, before the discharge instructions to wake the boy every two hours, before the businessman slips from our lives like a lost ticket stub, before the boy recovers and goes on to have dates and kids of his own—a daughter and younger son—and before the hypersonic trip through four decades, there is a piercing moan that can only come from the dark galaxy of a mother's lungs.

White Lies

Arpi, a Lebanese girl who pronounced *ask* as *ax* no matter how many times the teacher corrected her, must have been delighted by the arrival of Connie, the new girl in our fifth-grade class. Connie was albino, exceptionally white even by the ultra-Caucasian standards of our southern suburb. Only her eyelids had color: mouse-nose pink, framed by moth-white lashes and brows.

We had been taught that there was no comparative or superlative for *different*. Things were either different or the same, the teacher said. Likewise for *perfect*—something was either perfect or not. But surely Arpi thought of Connie as *more different* than herself. Arpi may have had a name that sounded all too close to Alpo, a brand of dog food, but at least she had a family whose skin and hair and eyes looked like hers. Connie, by comparison, was alone in her difference. She was, perhaps, *most different. Differentest.*

This was confirmed by the ridicule, which was immediate and unrelenting: *Casper, Chalk Face, Q-Tip.* Connie, whose shoulders hunched in a permanent parenthesis, pretended not to hear the names or the taunting questions: *What'd ya do, take a bath in bleach? Who's your boyfriend—Frosty the Snowman?* She sat in the front of the classroom, and if she felt the boys plucking white hairs from her scalp, she didn't react. The teacher, who was serving the last nine months of a thirty-year sentence in the public school system, spent the bulk of each day perusing magazines and L.L. Bean catalogs in the back of the room. As far as I know, she never intervened.

All of this changed in mid-October when Connie's father got a job at a candy factory, news Connie announced tentatively one rainy day during indoor recess.

Can he get us candy?

Yes.

Any kind? As much as we want? For free?

Yes, yes, yes.

And so the daily ritual began. Kids placed orders for Reese's Cups, Baby Ruth bars, Hubba-Bubba bubble gum. Connie kept a log of the requests in a pocket-sized notebook. The next day, she would tote a box full of candy into the classroom and distribute the promised sweets to eager hands. Overnight, Connie became the center of attention. Girls—even Marcia Miller, the first in our class to wear mascara—would beg to sit by Connie at lunch so they could update their orders.

And what about me? What was my role? Did I request my favorites—Three Musketeers and coconut-centered Mounds bars? Or did

I, as I have told myself and others in the years since, refuse to contribute to such cruelty? Or, in a more likely scenario, did I dump out my loot triumphantly at home one afternoon, only to be scolded by my mother? I don't remember, my memory obscured, I'm sure, by the wishful image of myself as a precocious champion of social justice. And I don't remember if I actually witnessed—or just imagined—Connie and her mother at the 7-Eleven one day after school. They were in the candy aisle. Her mother was filling a cardboard box. And Connie, bathed in unflinching fluorescence, was curved over her notebook making small, careful check marks.

Something for Everything

The woman at the next table in this strip mall sushi restaurant is trying to lure two young men into her sales scheme. She starts with the supplements she's taking. "I've lost 13 inches overall," she says. "*Inches.*"

"That's a lot of inches," they agree.

"It's all in the collagen," she tells them.

"Collagen," they repeat, trying out the word in their own mouths.

She has the high-pitched voice of one of their peers though she's old enough to be their mother. She knows them somehow. Maybe they live in her neighborhood or went to school with her daughter. She asks about their music, and one shows her the demo CD he's brought along.

"We're hoping to sit in with a band that tours all over," he says. "Well, they don't tour exactly, but they play a lot of local gigs."

We are sitting in a gated outdoor area, the only customers willing to brave the vague weather. The clouds are gray brushstrokes against the sky—they could go either way. The waiter is about their age. His name is Nathan. I take note because that's our own son's name. This Nathan sounds British, and when the woman says, "Oh Nathan, I love your accent—are you from Scotland?" he admits he's from right here in Middletown, Delaware.

Would our Nathan fake a foreign accent to pass the time on a job? Would he accept an invitation to dinner from someone who wants to tell him about "an exciting opportunity?" I don't know. I don't think so, but I just don't know. When the waiter leaves, the guys want to talk about him.

"That was random," one of them says, and the other adds, "Yeah, what the…"

But the woman reels them back to her script. She's just started using the shampoo. "Feel my hair," she insists, raving about its thickness and sheen. And there's laundry detergent—"My clothes have never been so clean!"—and a heart supplement. Again, it's all about the collagen. "They make something for everything," she purrs.

Here comes the pitch: the investment is just $39.95, and the earning potential is "limitless."

"Limitless," she repeats, aiming her key fob at the parking lot where the lights on a silver Lexus sedan blink on and off. "And when you pick up your orders at the warehouse, they fill your car with all kinds of products for you to try."

I've known acquaintances who hosted jewelry and kitchen parties. My cousin sold loungewear that looked like motel modern art paintings had melted onto fabric. A semi-complete list of the items I've bought during evenings of Chardonnay and Boursin cheese: a necklace with an off-center burnt-orange stone; herb scissors with their own teethed cleaner that resembles a tiny green Barbie comb; print yoga pants with a red splotch in the crotch that makes it look like I just started my period, though this has not been an issue for years.

When I was in junior high, the mom of a kid on my brother's soccer team was constantly pushing her cosmetic line. She'd charge up to me in the bleachers, grab a fistful of my cheek, and blurt, "Yup, I see a blemish! Is it almost your time of the month?"

The sky is growing darker. Every so often, the manager sticks his head out the door and looks up. Perhaps he wants us to offer to move inside. But my husband and I are comfortable in the slight September breeze as SUVs squeeze into spaces and mothers steer kids into Great Clips for back-to-school haircuts.

When the young men arrived, they came straight to the courtyard but didn't see the gate. One swung up his leg to climb over until the woman said, "Oh honey, just lift that latch right there." A part of me wanted to see him scale the wrought-iron fence, maybe take a running start and clear it like a hurdle at a track meet. There was something refreshingly innocent and reckless and sweet about the way he thought he needed to get from A to B.

Hotel, Hotel

Hotel, Hotel says the inn's hand-painted sign. My mother, college on hold, counts her *lire*, leaves a note for her sleeping husband, and kisses me— just half a year and tucked into my dresser-drawer crib—before setting off to find a market. A list-maker since she could grip a fat pencil in grade school, she is checking off *Tour Europe*. Back in Rhode Island, her parents' dreams rarely crossed the border of their factory town. They refused to sign papers for financial aid—*nobody's business how much money we make*—and distrusted anyone with a diploma.

On my mother's list this morning: fruit, baby food, a couple of the biscuits my father loved in Florence. She heads down a hill, turns here, dog-legs there. In the market she finds small jars with pictures of peaches and smiling babies, a can of tuna for lunch. She is proud to have managed without reading Italian, proud of the exchange with the grocer —*buon giorno, buon giorno*—and with this pride, a surge: she can do anything, go anywhere. Freshman year she'd caught the scent of rebellion drifting from the West Coast and gladly traded in her buttoned-up blazers for jeans and hand-knit shawls, convincing my father to shed his penny loafers and Catholic school rules over the objections of his mother, who'd fed him a lifetime worth of praise he didn't deserve. But these are sentences that will come years later.

For now, she is repeating *Hotel, Hotel?*, asking passersby to help retrace her steps. *Si, si,* they say, directing her to other inns, all with *hotel* signs. Up hills, down hills, through alleys—for hours she searches. Sobbing, her breasts milk-heavy, she thinks of her daughter waking hungry, the daughter who'd come earlier than they'd planned, the one who will realize this on her own when she's old enough to do the math. *Hotel, Hotel?* She may as well be asking for *il cielo*, the sky. She knows her husband will not change the baby's diaper. He will not think to let her gnaw on the bread leftover from last night's dinner.

There is much she doesn't know: that the tuna is actually cat food. That her marriage is short-lived. That once she's finished school, this story will become her song—*Hotel, Hotel* its refrain. It must have been early afternoon when she stumbled into the room, her cheeks tear-streaked. In my version, though, it's dusk. Shops are long shuttered. She is hungry to hold me. The empty streets echo my name.

A Lake of One's Own

When we arrived at Bear Creek Lake, the sky was clear, the Virginia sun scolding. It was the same state park where we'd been camping the previous year and learned, upon reemerging in civilization, that Elvis had died. Holding the front page of the *Richmond Times Dispatch*, my mother crumbled like a used tissue. I was too young to understand that Elvis was the youth she was losing, the carefree years before she was a divorced single mother supporting two children on a teacher's salary.

This late summer day, the typically crowded parking lot was empty. We unloaded our cooler packed with bottles of Coca Cola and cheese sandwiches and walked down to the beach. In the water, a staked sign announced that there was no swimming that day. Only it said "No Swiming," with one "m."

"Come on. Let's swim," my mother said.

We stripped down to our bathing suits. I waded freely into the roped-off area where I usually had to dodge the elbows of other kids. My brother toddled along the shallow part. My mother stood knee-deep watching us, reaching down periodically to douse her arms and chest. She was wearing a maroon one-piece suit with a wrap front. Despite her thin build, she never wore a bikini. "Women over thirty shouldn't show their bellies," she told me once.

Soon a gravel-spitting Jeep arrived, and a park ranger resembling a grown-up Boy Scout charged toward us.

"Excuse me!" he yelled.

"Yes?" my mother replied innocently.

"There's no swimming today! Can't you read the sign?"

"That sign?" my mother asked, pointing.

The ranger nodded. "Yes, ma'am. That sign. It says 'No Swimming.'"

"No, it says 'No Swiming,'" she said, emphasizing the long *i*. "See? One 'm.'"

The ranger looked at the sign, then back to my mother, then back to the sign again. If there was a reason the lake was closed—fecal coliform, state funding cuts—he didn't explain.

On the kitchen table back home, there were letters from my father's lawyer demanding money for his half of the house, even though, as my mother was quick to mention, his years of graduate school and unemployment meant he'd never contributed to the mortgage. Fearful we'd lose our home, my mother had interviewed to be a live-in nanny for a widowed businessman who traveled. If she got the job, the three of us would move into the finished attic above his daughters' rooms with their canopy beds and Princess phones.

"Sir," my mother said, her hand pressed earnestly to her chest. "I promise we won't swime."

The ranger shook his head and smiled. "Okay then," he said and walked away.

And so we swam. Reader, we swam.

Slow Burn

The day my brother nearly burns down the house, I am sitting on the living room floor.

Correction: it's not a house but an apartment, my father's first since the divorce.

I am playing with Lincoln Logs on the burnt-orange shag carpet, building and rebuilding a perfect house with a green roof.

Correction: I'm not playing; I'm killing time until we're returned to our real home with our real toys and our real parent.

My father is taking a nap in the apartment's only bedroom.

Correction: It's not a nap but his usual stupor, a label for which we won't have for years.

I see the fire out of the corner of my eye.

Correction: What I see first is the shadow puppet of a fire performing on the kitchen wall; mesmerized, I watch for the better part of a minute before investigating its cause.

When I crane my neck around the corner, I see my two-year-old brother waving a brown paper bag that he has dipped in the lit burner of the gas stove. *Pretty,* he exclaims. *Pretty! Pretty!*

Correction: He can't pronounce pretty. He says pity.

I knock the burning bag from my brother's hand and scream for our father, who bolts from the bedroom and douses the flames.

Correction: Our father doesn't respond until I shake him awake; he extinguishes the fire with a pot of cold, two-day-old coffee.

My brother's exclamations soften to a whisper: *Pity. Pity. Pity.*

No correction necessary.

Our Kitchens, Ourselves

My mother invented the twenty-minute meal. Or least she'd like credit for it, just as she'd like credit—or better yet, royalties—for aluminum foil pouches and the Holly Hobby doll, though neither invention at this point would let her quit her day job. But this was the 1970s: pre-microwave, post-June Cleaver, mid-cigarettes and single parenthood.

All of our appliances came from Sears Scratch 'n' Dent: brown refrigerator, white stove, avocado-green dishwasher, all of their dings camouflaged by strategically-placed magnets. Inside one kitchen cabinet were our coveted superhero drinking glasses—Wonder Woman for me, Batman for my younger brother. Inside another cabinet, my mother had taped a magazine photo of Robert Redford. "A woman can dream," she'd say. And it was always "woman"—never "girl" or "lady."

My mother dangled a Salem Menthol from her mouth as she stirred the simmering ground beef, adding a pouch of McCormick's "brown sauce" powder. In another wobbly pot, instant mashed potatoes congealed in a thin paste. Next came the layering: first the meat, then canned peas, then what my mother called "the starch"—a working mother's Shepherd's Pie. The whole dish was popped under the broiler for a minute or two until the top turned crusty. Before we set the table, we'd clear the day's newspapers—both morning and evening editions— and on weekends, we'd stack the lesson plans, mimeographs, student essays, and multiple choice quizzes (the latter of which I was permitted to help grade with my own red pen). The table was octagonal, designed and built by my mother in an evening woodworking class. It fit neatly in the corner of our small eat-in kitchen, the dining room having been converted to a bedroom for my brother. Against the wall, the table was the perfect size for the three of us. For company, we could pull it out and seat eight, as long as we kept our elbows tucked in at our sides.

Our kitchen wallpaper was better suited to a banker's study: repeated maps of the world in dark green and burgundy. My chair was next to Australia and New Zealand, two of the places my mother hoped one day to see. And the chair itself: high-backed with a straw seat that crunched each time I shifted. The bottom rung was the ideal place to hook my heels. On my birthday, my mother would wrap two empty Pringles cans in Reynolds Wrap, impale them on the chair's posts, and call it my throne.

My mother's other time-saving recipes: potato soup, chili, and a marinara that yielded three spaghetti dinners and two nights of sausage sandwiches. No matter the meal, we had cranberry sauce as a side dish, a holdover from her New England childhood. Sometimes there were

Brown 'n' Serve rolls, though usually we'd forget about them until we smelled them burning. It seemed there was always a saucepan of stewed tomatoes on the stove, though I don't remember ever eating them.

My mother had a boyfriend back then. She didn't call him her boyfriend, though; she called him her "friend." He had a motorcycle and a beard down to his navel. He brought steaks and broiled them in our oven late at night. The smell drifted under my door and up to the canopy bed I had bought with my own money. He never ate with us. He arrived well after dark, after my brother and I were asleep. Stewed tomatoes, travel, love—so many things my mother kept on the back burner.

Into the Answer

after Rilke

Your high school teacher mother taught you a trick for taking comprehension tests: always skip ahead to read the questions before the passage.

(Why are the mother's hands discolored?)

You remember her sitting at the kitchen table, her pen pressing deep into triplicate mimeograph sheets, the edges of her hands bruised with blue ink. Sometimes she'd let you grade her students' papers—yes, the way Tom Sawyer "let" the other boys whitewash Aunt Polly's picket fence.

(Why not "circumlocution" or "interpolate"?)

You loved making red checks and Xs for the root of "salubrious" or the Italian city where *Romeo and Juliet* was set.

(Why "first"?)

It was in a classroom that she had her first heart attack. A mother yourself by then, you weaned your toddler daughter on the spot to stay three nights on a hospital cot by her bedside, interrogating the cardiologist about circulation and stents and contraindications.

(Is daughter ever a verb?)

She insisted on slipping you bites of applesauce and poached chicken from her cafeteria tray, then tucked the heart attack in her pocket like a secret and taught another decade. Once a student asked if she had any Neosporin, and she joked, "I'll have you know I was once quite a looker, not some old lady with antibiotic cream in her purse."

(When does a mother stop mothering?)

As your grandma was dying, she motioned for your mother—then 70— to come close, perhaps for a kiss or to whisper words of wisdom or love. Instead, in her last breaths, she tugged up the zipper on your mother's fleece pullover, signaling that it was too lowcut. This is the gesture that caught in your mother's chest.

Something I Need to Tell You

The homemade rolls at the Chesterfield Inn were yeasty heaps of buttery heaven, kneaded and punched and baked by the staff whose uniforms matched the white linen tablecloths and napkins. Upstairs lived the wealthy elderly white women of Richmond who dined under the restaurant's antique chandeliers. They were not the kind of women to cook for themselves. They were the kind of women who "took their meals in the dining room." Despite its adornments, the Chesterfield was quite reasonably priced. You could get a three-course southern home-style meal for $6, which was inexpensive even in the mid-1980s. So one rainy Thursday evening, my friend Carrie and I—our driver's licenses freshly laminated—drove downtown for dinner.

Carrie, modeling herself after Madonna, had long blond hair that she spiked up in the front. She was partial to leggings under skirts, and layers of knit shirts and sweaters with gaping neck holes that exposed a shoulder. A few months earlier, we'd gone with a group of other girls to New York for the weekend. We'd piled into a single hotel room and spent the night dancing in the three-story club frequented by Madonna in *Desperately Seeking Susan*. That was the year of the first budget airline, and for $29 each way, we had flown to the city from Virginia Beach, where we stayed overnight before our early morning flight. It was at the beach that Carrie met a boy. Like the other Madonna, my friend was a virgin. As she put it, she was "saving herself" for marriage. She and the boy dressed in each other's clothes and romped around the off-season beach town until dawn.

That this boy would become her husband we didn't yet know. We were high school seniors. A part-time job and reading assignments for Ms. Saunders' Honors World Literature course consumed the bulk of my hours. Carrie spent most of her time tending to her invalid father, who was in his sixties when he'd married her much younger mother. They had since divorced, and it seemed he had been on the verge of death all the years I'd known Carrie. When he finally died later that year, Carrie made a quilt of his flannel pajamas. She said it smelled like him.

At the Chesterfield, we put our napkins on our laps. We sipped our iced tea. And when Carrie leaned forward and said, "There's something I need to tell you," I remember thinking this was still part of our grown-up role-playing.

She was nine. It was a family reunion. She'd wandered away from the crowd to a nearby neighbor's swing set. A man—a stranger—lured her into the woods. Her family members—absorbed in their hamburgers and horseshoes—could not hear her screams.

If I were writing fiction and said what I'm about to say, you would tell me it's not believable. *Too convenient*, you would say. But here it is: just weeks before my dinner with Carrie, Ms. Saunders—in one of her periodic rants that took flight from the books we were discussing—removed her reading glasses and gave us advice.

"If you are ever having dinner with a close friend and he or she tells you something important, something that is difficult and painful to tell," she said, pausing at the podium to wipe the air with her long arms, "here is what you *don't* do: you don't finish your meal. You get up from the table, leave your food, leave all of your money behind if you have to, and you go somewhere private and give that person your undivided attention."

I remember at the time thinking that Ms. Saunders must have been speaking from recent personal experience, but she didn't elaborate. Repositioning her glasses on the edge of her nose, she returned to *Madame Bovary* and asked, "So where were we?"

Our meals were served: country fried steak seeped in grease, three different kinds of venereal disease, macaroni and cheese with a thick scab of broiled cheddar, pelvic exam with a full-sized speculum, Hanover tomatoes stewed in their own juices, a girl's squeaky replies on the witness stand, the clinking of refilled iced tea glasses, the judge nudging her to *Speak up, please,* another basket of steaming rolls, the body weighted like a plumb line, chocolate pecan brownies with fresh whipped cream, the parole hearing, the fumbling with check and tip, the deep heat of shame—hers, and all these years later, mine.

pər(-ə)l

What do you think of first? The beads your boarding school classmates snatched from your throat to rub against their teeth? A test: were they real pearls or a $5 strand from Gordmans? Were you a real student or the daughter of a single mother on scholarship?

Or perhaps you think of *purl*, the inverted knitting stitch. From the Middle English: *pirl*, to twist. Like the time your mother was knitting a scarf to bring you for Parents' Weekend until her needles were confiscated by airport security. Cigarettes had just been banned on planes, so your single, smoking mother had nothing to do with her hands on the four-hour flight.

[This is a lie. Well, not the part about the knitting needles—it's true they were taken, though you don't remember where your mother was flying or what she was knitting. But she never came for Parents' Weekend. It was too far, too expensive. Your roommate's parents took you to Lowery's, the local seafood place where fried clams and shrimp came in red plastic baskets. Years later, you saw a photo of Lowery's in a book about Jim Crow. The sign said *We Serve Whites Only*.]

Maybe you think of Minnie Pearl, the comedian on *Hee Haw* with a permanent price tag dangling from her hat. You could have bought a new taffeta dress for the spring formal, tucked the tag inside the sleeve and returned it the next day. Instead, you wore a lace dress discarded from the school theatre costume closet. You dyed it with RIT powder in the laundry room sink, pink swirling like blood in the dorm toilet those times you crammed tissue in your panties and waddled down the hall to borrow a tampon.

[Do you distrust me now that you know I lied? Or do you trust me more because I admitted it?]

Or Pearl, daughter of Hester, the original single mother. You read *The Scarlet Letter* in Mrs. Perkins' 10th grade English class. Later that year, without telling you, she submitted a short story you wrote to a writing contest sponsored by the local community college. She surprised you with a first place certificate and $100 check, which she cashed for you because you didn't have a bank account.

You might picture the abalone ashtray your mother kept even after she stopped smoking. Home on summer break, you'd run your finger along its iridescent belly.

[*Iridescent:* a word you tell your students not to use. *Show me iridescence,* you say.]

Or maybe you think of an oyster at the bottom of the Chesapeake Bay. When an intruder—a parasite or piece of sand—penetrates the lips of its shell, the oyster coats it with a secretion—*nacre*—until it hardens like bone. Sometimes a shimmering sheath, sometimes a pearl. Something from nothing.

And which one are you, the oyster or the pearl? First or second person? I or you? Or I and you. Oyster and pearl. Mine and hers. I and you and oyster and pearl and mother-of-pearl and sand and water and blood and brine and truth and lies and mouth and tongue and words and words and words.

How to Make a Sugar Sandwich

If I knew more about cars, I could tell you the exact Mercedes Benz model Clarissa received for her 16th birthday. But I can recall only that it was silver, with leather interior, a sunroof, and an impressive cassette deck sound system on which we blasted the just-released Police album *Synchronicity*. As automobiles go, it may as well have been a different species from my family's radio-less orange Pinto station wagon with its four-speed manual transmission and "If you can read this, thank a teacher" bumper sticker.

Clarissa was one of my friends from the all-girls boarding school where I was on scholarship. I was visiting her in rural Virginia the August before my sophomore year. Clarissa was a year older and was as wealthy as we were poor. Her family's sprawling estate overlooked a lake. In the center of the compound was a swimming pool with a diving board and a slide, my childhood definition of heaven. On one side was the main house where her parents lived with her two younger brothers; on the other side was the guesthouse where Clarissa stayed when she was home from school. The guesthouse was the size and style of my family's home. It was a brick ranch with two bedrooms, a kitchen, bath, laundry room, and living room, the walls of which were lined with Clarissa's horseback riding trophies and ribbons. Her master bedroom had a walk-in closet where Clarissa showed me two dozen dresses she'd gotten in New York City earlier that summer, their price tags still dangling from sleeves. Wandering around her cottage, as she called it, I fantasized about living there myself, with my own phone line, cable television, and a wardrobe straight from the pages of a fashion magazine. Clarissa was clearly the luckiest girl on earth.

The main house was so large that I can't even reconstruct it in my mind. I remember the sauna in her parents' master bath and the gold-plated faucets on every sink. There was one other memorable detail: in the kitchen was a large scale, the kind I'd seen only in doctor's offices. It wasn't until later in the week that I learned its purpose.

Up until then, our relationship had existed independently of family. Like me, Clarissa was an honors student, which meant that while most of our classmates attended mandatory study hall after dinner, we had "privileges." We could play tennis or walk to town or watch TV in the social room. Mostly, though, we hung out in each other's dorm rooms reading and listening to music. Clarissa wasn't the type to reveal much about her personal life; she preferred to talk more abstractly about books or celebrities.

The first evening of my visit, Clarissa's parents summoned us into their bedroom where they were watching TV. The room was like a luxury hotel suite with its silk and chintz décor. They motioned for us to sit on the foot of the overstuffed bed. What did my parents do, they wanted to know. My parents were divorced, I said, and my father was a social worker, which was true enough. I didn't mention that he was quickly slipping away into the mental illness that would eventually claim his job, his home, and his connection with reality. My mother was a safer subject. She was a teacher. But when I told them she had spent most of her career in an inner-city high school in Richmond, Clarissa's father seemed to relish the opportunity to trot out his favorite racist jokes, all of which left me stunned and none of which deserves to be retold here. Her mother smiled tightly. Clarissa bristled. I did not tell them that my mother was forced to work second and third jobs, that we lived with the constant threat of having our utilities cut off, that some days I had nothing but sugar sandwiches to pack for lunch.

Later that night, back in her cottage, Clarissa explained that the man I'd met was actually her stepfather. Her father had left when she was a child, and her mother had remarried the wealthy man who had adopted her. The boys were her half-brothers. She hadn't seen her biological father in years; the only thing she knew was that he had served in the military, Vietnam perhaps, though she didn't say so.

There wasn't much to do in the sleepy town. We spent the days lounging by her pool. At night, we drove down windy back roads with the windows and sunroof open, wailing along with the stereo: "Since you've gone I've been lost without a trace/I dream at night/I can only see your face…" Oh, how we loved Sting, with his wispy blonde hair and intellectual lyrics about Scylla and Charybdis and Mephistopheles. One night we stopped at a convenience store where the local teenagers hung out in the parking lot. But Clarissa didn't know these kids, and besides, her car didn't exactly fit in with their jacked-up Camaros. We strolled in for slushies and walked slowly back to her car, all the while eyeing the girls in tank tops and cut-off shorts who leaned on the boys' bumpers. Clarissa was quiet on the ride home.

Each morning when I awoke, Clarissa was gone. When she returned, she'd say she'd been talking to her mother. One morning, I wandered up to the main house and into the kitchen. Clarissa was on the scale and her mother was yelling, "What did you eat? Are you *trying* to turn into a pig?" Clarissa sobbed, "But I'm about to start my period, Mom!" Both seemed startled to see me, but her mother continued. "You'll never find a man looking like that, missy."

I had never experienced anything quite like this. Clarissa wasn't overweight by anyone's standards, though she wasn't thin like her mother, a brittle bird of a woman with dyed dark brown hair and enough make-up to add a pound or two to her own weight. When I had come home from my first year of boarding school a good eight pounds heavier—thanks to the deep-fried Southern fare of the dining hall—my mother had gently suggested we do a two-week diet together, even though she didn't need to slim down. But never once had she berated me about my size or my food choices.

I left boarding school after that year and soon lost touch with Clarissa. I assumed that she, like many of my classmates, had gone on to college for her "MRS degree," as the joke went (Even the lyrics to commencement's "Pomp and Circumstance" were altered by students to fit this theme: "I want to get married/I want to be a wife/I want to get married/I'm sick of this boarding school life.").

Years later, I met someone else who reminded me so much of Clarissa that, to this day, I sometimes confuse them in my mind. The new "Clarissa" was my co-worker at a newspaper where I was an editor and she was a photographer. Ally was smart like Clarissa and looked a little like her. But there was something more subtle that connected them. Eventually I learned that Ally's older brother—her only sibling—had been hit and killed by a drunk driver when he was a teenager. It was the middle of the day, and he'd been riding his bike home from a friend's house. For half her life, Ally had tried, impossibly, to be both son and daughter to her parents. That was the similarity: the sadness just below the surface, the loneliness that comes from living in an echo chamber of someone else's unresolved resentments and grief.

The last night of my stay at Clarissa's house, we were driving around town when she said, "I'm sorry about the whole weight thing."

"It's not your fault," I offered.

She went on to explain the daily routine. Every morning, she had to report for "weigh-in," and if she was just a few ounces heavier than the day before—113.3 pounds versus 113, say—her mother would scold her mercilessly. "It makes me so mad," Clarissa said. But it didn't seem like anger to me. Suddenly, Clarissa's magical cottage felt more like a gilded prison.

To make a sugar sandwich, you'll need two pieces of white bread (not wheat or whole grain); margarine (not butter); and white granulated sugar. [Warning: be sure the margarine tub—which makes for a good Tupperware substitute—is, indeed, filled with hydrogenated oil and not mashed potatoes left over from last night's dinner.] Slather the bread with margarine, then sprinkle a layer of sugar on top. Take the sandwich outside and perch on the front step while your younger brother rumbles up and down the sidewalk on his Big Wheel. Soon your mother will call from her night bartending job to make sure you've put the laundry in the dryer. "Thanks, sweetie. Love you," she'll say, as always, before hanging up. Now take a bite of your sandwich. Your fingertips glisten with the sugar's silver glitter. And it tastes rich, but not too rich. Just rich enough.

For Deirdre, the Cocktail Waitress Who Bought My Book

When you come over to greet us, I can see it in your eyes: Great—I got the poetry section. Bet they're good tippers. But you don't say this; instead you say, "Hi, my name's Deidre, and I'll be taking care of you."

I've worked in enough bars to know that a place that's lively and festive at night can become a dank and depressing shell of itself in the splintered light of day. This one is no different. The tables are sticky with beer residue. The well smells like wet towels. And even though smoking has been banned in this city for years, the air holds onto a haze like a grudge.

It's usually only the truly committed drinkers who shuffle in on a Saturday afternoon. But today, even without the fellow writers we've dragged along as our audience, there are a dozen folks propped on bar stools, most of them men. When we start testing the microphone—*one, two, three*—a few swivel around out of curiosity.

You're wearing the same zippered apron I wore as a cocktail waitress: big enough to fit your tips and check pad, small enough to blend with your black jeans. The apron starts out light, but as the shift progresses, you can gauge how well you're doing by the weight around your hips.

I'm going to guess you're in your early twenties, though I have to admit that the farther I get from that decade, the harder it is for me to judge. You've got smoky eye shadow and a barrette pinning back your bangs. When I was your age, I spent a summer working in a bar not far from here. Hal, the owner, was a white American man married to a Thai woman who had her own upscale restaurant across the street. I swear she bought the bar just to keep him out of her hair. She wore tailored silk suits and made her husband drive her to work in a limousine, the license plate of which boasted the name of her restaurant.

My boss was a relaxed, jovial guy when his wife wasn't around, but as soon as she strode through the door with her entourage of assistants—something we learned could happen at any minute—he snapped to attention. Susie was her name. It was also the way she referred to herself, always in third person. *Susie not happy with silverware, Ellen,* she would say, mispronouncing my name. Even my co-workers began calling me Ellen. It started as a way to mock Susie, but with the turnover typical of restaurants, the joke was lost on newcomers. Soon, it was my new name.

After a while, I even began introducing myself to customers as Ellen. It was just as well—in an environment of feigned intimacy, it helped to remind myself I was playing a role, smiling at stupid jokes, flirting with big spenders. Prostitution may be illegal, but when your income depends on tips, there's a fine line between doing your job and selling yourself. With single men, I never mentioned my boyfriend. *You got it, girlfriend*, I'd say to tables of women enjoying ladies' night out. With older couples, it helped to mention that I was a college student. I never told anyone I wanted to be a writer.

One night another customer and I drove a regular home. He was recently divorced and had had a few too many. The other customer drove the drunk guy's car with him in it, and I followed behind in mine. We steered him down the steps to his one-room basement apartment. Flush with the ceiling were two windows the size of shoe boxes. When we settled him on his sofa bed, he offered us a drink. *Thanks, no*, we said, and I drove the other man back to the bar to pick up his own car.

Another night I babysat for a female customer who came into the bar by herself several nights a week. She never had more than a glass of wine; her mission was to meet a man. She lived in a high-rise that overlooked the park below. *Alimony,* she said, when I admired the view. I could tell she'd once been attractive, but now she wore too much make-up and stuffed herself into outfits two sizes too small, like the sheer white knit top and short skirt she was wearing that evening, her belly spilling over the waistband. Her four-year-old son snuggled up next to me and begged me to tell him stories. Around two a.m., she came home alone, her mascara smeared.

The bartender, Phil, filled my drink orders at one end of the bar, the overflow sloshing onto a rubber mat. During slow periods, I'd pull up a stool there, and we'd banter about sports, current events, or the antics of the night before. I'd heard from a longtime waitress that Phil was a recovering alcoholic who frequently fell off the wagon. Once he came in on his night off with two other men and installed himself at the bar. He was doing shots, and it didn't take long before he was slamming each small glass down and demanding another. Just before closing, he called me over. *I want you to meet my friend*, he said. When I went to shake the hand of the man next to him, Phil grabbed a fistful of my hair at the roots and yanked my face down to his lap. *Give me a blow job*, he growled. The other men at the bar erupted with laughter. I pulled free and ran to the kitchen.

I wish I could tell you I quit that night. I wish I could tell you I spun out of the gravel parking lot in my blue Kharmann Ghia, leaving a cloud of dust in my wake. I didn't. I had two weeks left till the next semester started, and I was still four hundred dollars shy of the money I needed for tuition.

The next morning, I went into work and told Hal what had happened. He called Susie who marched across the street in her heels and asked me to repeat my story. She conferred with Hal in the back room and left.

Phil was suspended for three days. When he returned, I still had to put in my drink orders with him and wait at the end of the bar. He'd take his time, wiping and rewiping glasses before he'd pour each gin and tonic, vodka on the rocks, and—a customer favorite—Long Island Iced Tea. His first night back, he told me, *Thanks for the vacation. Me and my girlfriend rented a cabin in the mountains and had a blast.*

How nice for you, I answered, loading drinks onto my tray.

Hey, I brought you a souvenir, he said, and pulled a small giraffe from a shelf under the counter.

Look, its neck bends all the way down. See?

He pushed a button on the figurine's back and held it near his crotch. The giraffe bobbed up and down.

What's the matter, can't you take a joke? Phil asked with searing eyes.

My hands shook as I delivered the drinks to my tables, the glasses clinking like small bells.

Flash forward more than twenty years. I've finished college and graduate school, gotten married, had two children, published several books, gotten tenure. I'm giving a reading with two other women poets in this Irish pub, a different environment from the typical academic venues with their stiff chairs and fluorescent lighting. But the poet who coordinated the event grew up nearby and knew she'd attract more friends and family if they could drink while listening to poetry.

As I'm reading, I barely notice you weaving between tables, leaning over to solicit orders in a hushed voice. Afterwards, you bring a copy of my most recent book for me to sign. I'm used to the *I'll scratch your book, you scratch mine* reciprocity of writers, but you—you've worked hard for your tips. I'm honored that you spent a good portion of them on my poems.

On the drive home, I wonder what poem spoke to you. The one with the joke about the man's *dangling preposition*? Even the regulars laughed when I introduced the poem just as an ad for a popular erectile dysfunction drug appeared on the bar's jumbo TV screen. Or the one about the young boy selling his Matchbox cars? Perhaps you have a child of your own at home. Maybe it was the poem about the boarding school girls allowed to smoke Virginia Slims from dorm windows in exchange for baring their breasts to the night watchman—a poem about young women using their bodies as currency. In the end, I'm sure you noticed, the speaker realizes what she's worth.

In Case of Emergency

Where would *we live if you and Daddy died?* our daughter asks at dinner. Our teenage son looks up from his spaghetti-spooled fork, interested, for once, in something his younger sister has said. We are not planning to die anytime soon. But our daughter is good at questions. When she was two, she asked if a knife could cut another knife. At first, a digression: our son mentions foster care, wonders aloud if they'd have to change schools. Then my daughter says, *Yeah, and we'd have to take a special bus with the other kids of parents who died.* We run with this idea. *The Orphan Bus! It would be black! It would drive with its lights on all day like a hearse! All the other cars would pull over to let it pass!* But it's sweet, really, the thought that her loss would be so all-consuming that she'd have to segregate herself, unable even to engage in normal school bus banter. It occurs to me that she has barely been brushed by death. Even Romeo, her betta fish, has outlived our expectations. *If Daddy and I died,* I say, *Grandma and Grandpa would come to live with you. You wouldn't have to change houses or schools.* This is not something I have discussed with my mother and stepfather, but I feel certain they'd rise to the occasion. I watch my children roll this idea around in their minds. *Okay, so our parents are dead, but we get to keep the same bedrooms, same friends, same lockers at school,* they seem to be thinking. *But what if <u>they</u> die?* our daughter wants to know. I offer surrogate B. *And if she dies?* Surrogate C. *And if she dies?* I am quickly exhausting the list of people who would be willing, on a moment's notice, to drop their own lives, move to central/western Pennsylvania, and raise my kids. And here our son—who has already flirted with transformation, who finds hair sprouting in unexpected places, who sees his former Little League teammates toking joints behind the YMCA, who once watched a video of himself as a young boy and said, *Man, <u>this</u> me would hate <u>that</u> me*—here our son interrupts. *If she died,* he says, *we'd both be charged with murder 'cause everyone who lives with us ends up dead.* And he is right—not that he and his sister would be arrested, but that we should end this conversation, and we should end it laughing.

Lacy

Our son convinced us he was the only kid in fifth grade without a dog, and so that winter we got a Border Collie pup with a perfect white blaze between her eyes. There'd been a blizzard the week we brought her home, and she became conditioned to peeing in the snow. As temperatures rose, we had to wander farther and farther—sometimes at 3 a.m.—to find an unmelted patch under a shrub.

She'd sleep with Nathan in his loft and wait at the front window for the school bus each day, her nose smudging the glass like finger paints. A herder without a job—"unemployed," we dubbed her—she'd nudge us awake each morning and glower as we backed out of the drive. Such irredeemable sheep we were. Once she got loose and bolted more than a mile—Nathan trailing in bare feet—until a stranger opened a car door and beckoned her inside.

All these years later, my son is away at school, and Lacy's heart is failing. Today we took what was likely her last long walk. When we reached the hill by the cemetery, she slowed almost to a stop. I used to be the one who lagged behind, panting, as she sprinted ahead, tugging the leash taut. And now I pretend to prefer this pace, though we manage only two blocks an hour. She is a toddler taking her first tentative steps, lowering each foot as if at any moment the ground could turn to air, as if we have no place to be and all the time we need to get there.

Tanya the Phlebotomist

My newborn daughter had to have her blood drawn twice a day. High hemoglobin, the doctors said. Our hearts rose and fell with each result, with worry for what might come next.

Every morning and late afternoon, my husband drove us to the lab at our local hospital, Molly bundled in her infant car seat and me next to her cradling my stapled c-section wound. The first day multiple phlebotomists tried to tap into her tiny veins without success, leaving her arms and feet butchered and bruised. And then Tanya arrived, a young Black woman working in a part of Maryland where the KKK still held rallies, where just a few years earlier, a Black man was dragged from a car and beaten for riding with a white woman. Tanya cupped our daughter's heel in her hand and spoke her name—"Molly. Hi, sweet Molly"—and in one swift motion, threaded the needle and summoned a vial full of blood. Molly didn't cry. She didn't even stir.

Twice a day we saw her. Sometimes our daughter never woke up. Other times Tanya let her stay latched to my breast. We sensed tension when we told the other techs—all white—that we wanted to wait for Tanya. After a while, they wouldn't even greet us—they'd see us walk in and snap, "Tanya, you got a patient."

One day we showed up and Tanya was gone—working in another lab in the hospital that day, the tech on duty reported.

"Fine," my husband said, "we'll go there."

This wasn't an option, we were told, because that lab didn't take our insurance.

My husband—who hates confrontations—said "I don't care. I'll pay cash. No one but Tanya is touching my child."

That's when a supervisor was called, and Tanya was dispatched to work her magic on Molly. This continued for about a week until her condition resolved on its own.

Flash forward twenty years. We have moved to another state. My husband needs routine blood work, so we follow the GPS directions to a lab in a business park where we take a number and sit in the waiting room.

You know where this is going, don't you? The phlebotomist who takes his blood is Tanya. I recognize her all these years later, and she confirms that yes, she worked at that rural hospital back then, and yes, she was routinely called for babies and other challenging patients. She doesn't remember us, but who can blame her? She's had a million patients since then while we've had only a handful of people draw our blood.

She tells us she's worked in Georgia and spent five years traveling the country as a lab trainer. Her daughter who was in elementary school when we first met is a third-grade teacher now. And our daughter is pre-med, with flash cards for anatomy & physiology and a white coat and goggles for chemistry lab.

Tanya hasn't lost her touch. She taps his inner arm—the *antecubital fossa*, our daughter will tell me later—and glides the needle into his vein. She comments on his muscles, asks about his workout routine. She's running a half marathon this weekend, she tells us. She hopes it doesn't rain. And with that, her work is done. And he didn't feel a thing.

In/strum/ent

1.

I notice the word "strum" hiding in "instrument" and decide to see if they share a root. I search for the OED, but AutoCorrect changes it to Zoe.

2.

My husband's first wife has a daughter named Zoe. What the hell, I google my husband's first wife and find her wedding notice in the *Washington Post* and a quote in a parenting magazine (she makes most of the decisions and her second husband, a cardiologist, usually goes along).

3.

The Oxford English Dictionary, according to an online review, is recommended by 91% of readers. Are the other 9% objecting to English as the language of colonizers (legit) or opposed to words in general? Like, maybe they'd give air itself a 7 out of 10?

4.

I used "strum" in a poem once to describe a janitor jerking off in a parking lot:

> Smitty, the night watchman
> who let us boarding school girls
> smoke Virginia Slims
> from dorm-room windows
> as long as we bared our breasts…
> *Show Smitty some titty,*
> *show Smitty some titty*, a mantra
> he grunted under a streetlamp,
> one hand strumming below
> the belt of his blue uniform.

5.

Do I plagiarize myself? Very well then I plagiarize myself.

6.

I once asked a fourth-grade class what word was hiding in "personification." I was looking for the obvious—"person"—but a boy raised his hand and said "cat." He was not wrong ("litotes," a positive expressed through a negative). He was also most likely to become a poet.

7.

Another time, a kid on my son's Little League team said, "You write poems? I know how to spell onomatopoeia: O-N-O-M-A-T-O-P-O-E-I-A." I asked him if he knew what it meant, and he said, "Oh yeah, my uncle has a bad case of it." I imagined his uncle walking around like Adam West with Tourette's: *Bam! Pow! Splat!* Turns out he was confusing onomatopoeia with alopecia, a condition that causes hair loss.

8.

When I was twelve, my mother laughed when I vowed to marry a man who was a gourmet cook/masseur/guitarist. My husband makes a mean lasagna and rubs my shoulders without being asked, but he plays jazz piano, not guitar. We all have to make sacrifices, I like to joke.

9.

Remember the song "Killing Me Softly" made famous by Roberta Flack? The first line is "Strumming my pain with his fingers." Wikipedia tells me a 20-year-old woman named Lori Lieberman wrote it in 1971 (the year my husband married his first wife).

10.

My husband says there was little pain from their divorce. They were young, had no kids or joint property, and parted on friendly terms.

11.

Lori Lieberman was inspired by a Don McLean concert at the Troubadour in L.A.: "And there he was this young boy/ A stranger to my eyes." I prefer the lower, slower Fugees version, a breathy Lauryn Hill stripping it down over a hip hop thrum.

12.

"Thrum," I learn, is the root of strum, while "instrument" derives from the Anglo-Norman *enstrument*. So, no connection.

13.

One Christmas I walked into a record store—back when there were record stores—to buy an album for our daughter. "I can't remember the name," I told the shaggy salesclerk who'd been summoned from the stockroom. "But the reviewer described him as 'Van Morrison singing through two blades of grass.'" Without missing a beat, he said, "David Gray, aisle eight."

14.
"Strum (v.): to play carelessly or unskillfully." You can almost hear the scorn in the lexicographer's definition. Strumming is sloppy, unrefined—surely nothing worthwhile could come from such random sweeping gestures of the thumb or mind.

Tell Me Something You've Learned in the Past Two Days
#1 job interview question of the former VP of Human Resources at Microsoft

- That the cherry blossoms have reached peak bloom.

- That hand soap removes ketchup stains from clothing.

- That a whole industry wants me to worry about the scent of my vagina.

- That the word for cherry blossom, *Sakura,* comes from *saku* 咲, which also means "smile" and "laugh."

- That Heinz released a special edition condiment: Tomato Blood.

- That Gwyneth Paltrow wants me to buy a vagina-scented candle.

- That a Wisconsin school district banned a Dolly Parton song because it mentions rainbows.

- That the 口 in 咲 indicates an open mouth.

- That you can order a cherry blossom-scented douche from Amazon.com.

- That one of my students slit his wrists in eighth grade, convinced there was no place in this world for a gay Black man.

- That the gamers who designed *Call of Duty* met gun manufacturers at a shooting range in Nevada to record the precise sounds of AR-15s.

- That soap doesn't work on blood no matter how hard you scrub.

- That according to Google AutoComplete, the most commonly-searched questions include "Why are AR-15s legal?" and "Why are AR-15s so expensive?"

- That we should stop using the term "bullet points."

- That cherry blossoms symbolize the fleeting nature of life.

- That Nevada isn't pronounced with an "ah" but more nasally: "Nev*a*da," like the *a* in "ammunition" and "capitalism" and "casket."

Mother as Conjunction
Spring 2020

I've had daughters move home on their way from one frayed relationship to the unknown. The tear-swollen eyes. The packed hatchback, mauve bedspread smashed against the passenger window. This is different. Two of my grown children are here for the duration. Mother as noun. Mother as verb. Mother as conjunction.

***

How old were you when you learned *mauve* rhymes with *drove*? That *segue* is not spelled *segway*? That the bird you hear when you wake is a *mourning* dove, not a *morning* dove? How could you have ignored the sorrow in its song?

***

I've organized the spices in the lazy Susan, labels on top. Who was Susan and what made her lazy? It's all about the z sound, the sibilant. I arrange the jars alphabetically and turn them round and round: adobo, anise, basil, bay leaves, chervil, dill. A doctor friend is in charge of a COVID unit in New York City. They turn the patients like rotisserie chickens, draining quarts of sputum from their lungs.

***

The lieutenant governor of Texas says *Some things are more important than living.* I can only think of one thing.

***

Dream: we have to sleep on tree limbs, tensing our bellies to keep from spilling over the sides, afraid to drift off.

***

We are removed from the groove of consumerism, the fresh-purchase rush of a new plush throw in our ongoing attempt to create *hygge* ("hoo-gah"), the Danish word for coziness. We move our sluggish bodies, not spending but spent.

***

I don't know what I love more: forsythia's wild lion mane or the word *forsythia*, the way it coaxes the tongue from behind the teeth. In a typical spring there is a sudden eruption of yellow that just as quickly turns green. But this year I witness the gradual transition, each petal inched out by a leafy shoot. They say the virus might spread through aerosol. In a 60-person choir, 45 people fell ill, one member infecting the others through song. Say *forsythia, forsythia*—say it safely when you are alone.

***

I insist on rituals—coffee on the back porch—as if demanding a photo of my old self holding today's newspaper, proof of a former life. A robin assembles a nest in a hedge, layers it with twigs and grass. Soon there will be eggs the color of—*of Joan Baez's lover's eyes*, I joke because there is humor here in the architecture of the ordinary.

***

This is a good time to master the difference between *lie* and *lay*. Lie, lay, lain. Lay, laid, laid. Was I lying in bed or laying in bed when I heard the mourning dove? *People lie and chickens lay*, my teachers used to say. Faulkner: *As I Lay Dying*. The president lies. The president is lying.

***

All of the restaurants are dark. People break in, sleep on the booths, drink the booze, spoon mouthfuls of industrial-sized cans of soup. Our favorite sushi place has a red room reserved for overflow where they let us sit, even on a quiet Tuesday. The hostess doesn't ask—she just takes us to our favorite table in the corner, its vinyl seats repaired with duct tape. Above us, a framed print of Mount Fuji is covered in clingwrap to protect it from grease and dust. We've read that 70 percent of restaurants may not survive. The president says *They will come back. They may not be the same restaurants or the same owners, but they will come back.* Will people come back, too, but with different names and faces?

***

Dream: it's the last night at Carly's, the bar where I served cocktails in college. As a gift, Carly gives us cassette recordings of ourselves when we were young. I am 14 and talking about a book in my high school English class. I use the word *linear*. I barely recognize my own voice. That was the year I bit a wart off the base of my left index finger. I still have the scar. I go to thank Carly but can only hug myself.

***

Will there always be before and after? This is the orderly independent clause; the scattered shattered after is this.

***

The federal government ordered an extra 100,000 body bags this week. The dead are stacked in refrigerated trucks that hum through the night, a one-note lullaby droning in empty city streets.

***

We bathe in the sameness of days, soft water sliding over our skin like silicone. Is there a word for tedium tinged with fear? A man in a black mask leaves groceries at our door, rings the bell then disappears. The boxes are dusted with April snow. He has replaced bananas with butternut squash. Because they are both yellow or both start with *b*? I will never know.

Shaped

our life a time-shaped miracle
—Brenda Hillman

I should have paid attention in geometry instead of staring at the yellow patch in Mrs. Reid's snowy hair, wondering if a rodent had peed on her while she was sleeping.

***

I barely know what a parabola is, but I want to climb inside the word, slide down its sloped walls, skateboarder in a drainpipe of echoes. *Parabolic*, so close to *parable*, a lesson to be learned or ignored.

***

At nineteen I stayed on the eighth floor of the San Francisco YMCA, still a stranger in my own body, still trying to squeeze my curves into the square jeans I'd seen in glossy magazines. One morning in the group shower, another naked woman looked me up and down and said *Giiirl, you sure got a nice shape.*

***

My husband needs eye surgery to correct an earlier procedure. *Capsular haze*, they call the film that makes the world look like a fogged bathroom mirror. The doctor lasers a hexagon opening in the implanted lens. His brain interprets it as a circle.

***

Once in the school library, I saw Mrs. Reid emerge from the ladies' room, polyblend skirt smashed into the back of her pantyhose revealing a white rhombus of underwear. I did not warn her before she walked out into the gauntlet of students.

***

When my father-in-law was nearing ninety, he sat with my toddler son sorting plastic blocks into holes—red triangle into triangle hole, blue oval into oval hole. They were the same age, the decades atrophied by dementia. Frustrated, he snatched the pieces from my son's chubby hands and snarled, *I was playing first!* My husband said *Dad, he's just a baby.*

***

My friend whose son disappeared raises butterflies with stained glass wings. Her living room is full of tiny geodesic domes where just-hatched broods hunch like rain-soaked hitchhikers. Her favorite is Dolly, named for Dolly Parton. Born with a bent wing, she will never fly. My friend lets her roam the house, feeds her melons and honey water. Sometimes she swears she's lost and will search and search until she finds her atop a lampshade or an open book.

***

In my father-in-law's last days, his son became his father. *Papa, Papa* he would cry, time compressed. He would stroke the arc of his forehead and say *Don't worry* to calm him. *Don't worry.* A palimpsest of years and pronouns: *he* and *his* and *him. Their, their. There, there.*

***

Disappeared isn't the right word. My friend's son was kidnapped by her ex before he could say *Mama,* before faces on milk cartons, before genealogy kits and hi-tech tracking. He would be almost fifty now, twice the age she was when she last held him.

***

Picture Dolly's mouth when she sings *I will always love you-ooooo,* the notes from her lungs stretching like the bubble from a child's wand as he runs barefoot in grass.

***

Light-shaped. Fear-shaped. Loss-shaped. Vowel-shaped.

***

When my son was born, I buried my face into the fleshy origami of his neck and inhaled and inhaled and for the first time did not think about what came before or next, only the yeasty smell of his skin, the warm, doughy folds.

***

This-shaped. Now-shaped. The shape of what we carry, what we hold.

Acknowledgments

Works in this book appeared in the following publications, sometimes under different titles:

"Re-entry," *The Cincinnati Review.*

"Slow Burn" appeared originally in *Junk* and was reprinted in the following anthology:

> *Creating Nonfiction: Twenty Essays and Interviews with the Writers* (SUNY Press)

"White Lies" appeared originally in *Brevity* and was reprinted in the following publications:

> *The Best of Brevity* (Rose Metal Press)

> *Creative Nonfiction* magazine's Sunday Short Reads #20

> *Kept Secret: The Half-Truth in Nonfiction* (Michigan State University Press)

> *Wordsmith: A Guide to Paragraphs and Short Essays,* 6th edition (Pearson)

> *Models for Writers: Short Essays for Composition* 11th, 12th, 13th, 14th and 15th editions (Bedford/St. Martin's Press)

"Something for Everything," *Guesthouse.*

"pər(-ə)l," *Superstition Review.*

"Hotel, Hotel," *Marginalia.*

"A Lake of One's Own," *Black Box.*

"Our Kitchens, Ourselves," *Bluestem.*

"Something I Need to Tell You," *Barnstorm Journal.*

"For Deirdre, the Cocktail Waitress Who Bought My Book," *North American Review*.

"In Case of Emergency" appeared originally in *The Ilanot Review* and was reprinted in:

    Best Microfiction 2024 (Pelekinesis Press)

"In/strum/ent," *JMWW*.

"Tell Me Something You've Learned in the Past Two Days," *Litro*.

"Mother as Conjunction," *Bending Genres*.

"Shaped," *Raven's Perch*.

"White Lies" was nominated for a Pushcart Prize by *Brevity*.

Erin Murphy's work has appeared in *The Best of Brevity, Best Microfiction 2024,* and anthologies from Random House, Bloomsbury, and Bedford/ St. Martin's. Her most recent books are *Human Resources, Fluent in Blue,* and *Taxonomies.* Her edited anthologies include *Creating Nonfiction* and *Bodies of Truth: Personal Narratives on Illness, Disability, and Medicine,* both of which won Foreword INDIES Book of the Year Awards. She is professor of English at Penn State Altoona. Website: www.erin-murphy.com

About Small Harbor Publishing

Small Harbor Publishing is a 501c3 nonprofit organization. Our goal is to publish unique and diverse voices. We are a feminist press, and we are committed to diversity and inclusion. We strive to bring new voices to a devoted and expanding readership.

Small Harbor Publishing began in 2018 with the first issue of *Harbor Review*. The magazine is an online space where poetry and art converse. *Harbor Review* quickly grew and now publishes reviews and runs multiple micro chapbook competitions, including the Washburn Prize and the Editor's Prize.

In July 2020, Small Harbor Publishing was officially incorporated and began Harbor Editions. Harbor Editions accepts submissions through a chapbook open reading period, a hybrid chapbook open reading period, the Marginalia Series, and the Laureate Prize.

In 2023, Harbor Anthologies began with a mission to promote texts that explore social justice issues and highlight marginalized writers.

If you would like to support Small Harbor Publishing, visit our "About" page at: smallharborpublishing.com/about.

Made in the USA
Monee, IL
07 July 2026